Brief Notes

LEASING STRATEGIES

The publications in *Brief Notes* are outlines of core topics of interest to professionals involved in shopping center management. The outlines are capsule overviews of each topic. Many key points are covered, and shopping center examples are provided for further illustration. Core concepts in each area guide you on topics you may want to explore further. Each outline also contains a helpful glossary.

Brief Notes is designed to provide a helpful and informative overview of the topics covered. It is not intended to be a substitute for more extensive learning that can be achieved through attending ICSC educational programs and reading additional ICSC professional publications.

The outlines contained in *Brief Notes: Shopping Center Management:*

- Management Overview
- Finance
- Insurance and Risk Management
- The Lease and Its Language
- Leasing Strategies
- Maintenance
- Marketing
- Retailing
- Security

Brief Notes

LEASING STRATEGIES

 International Council of Shopping Centers
New York

ABOUT THE INTERNATIONAL COUNCIL OF SHOPPING CENTERS

The International Council of Shopping Centers (ICSC) is the trade association of the shopping center industry. Serving the shopping center industry since 1957, ICSC is a not-for-profit organization with over 44,000 members in 77 countries worldwide.

ICSC members include shopping center

- owners
- developers
- managers
- marketing specialists
- leasing agents
- retailers
- researchers
- attorneys

- architects
- contractors
- consultants
- investors
- lenders and brokers
- academics
- public officials

ICSC sponsors more than 200 meetings a year and provides a wide array of services and products for shopping center professionals, including deal making events, conferences, educational programs, accreditation, awards, publications and research data.

For more information about ICSC, write or call the
International Council of Shopping Centers
1221 Avenue of the Americas
New York, NY 10020-1099
Telephone: 646-728-3800
Fax: 212-589-5555
info@icsc.org
http://www.icsc.org

This publication is designed to provide accurate and authoritative information in regard to the subject matter covered. It is sold with the understanding that the publisher is not engaged in rendering legal, accounting, or other professional services. If legal advice or other expert assistance is required, the services of a competent professional person should be sought.

> —*From a Declaration of Principles jointly adopted by a Committee of the American Bar Association and a Committee of Publishers.*

Companies, professional groups, clubs and other organizations may qualify for special terms when ordering quantities of more than 20 of this title.

Published by
International Council of Shopping Centers
Publications Department
1221 Avenue of the Americas
New York, NY 10020-1099
ICSC Catalog No.: 242
ISBN: 1-58268-028-0

Contents

Preface

Leasing is the middle step that takes a retail development from a construction project to an operating retail entity.

Leasing is people to people. It is options. It is alternatives. It's having a product that retailers want to be part of and creating a retail environment which shoppers want to be part of.

Leasing is an art and it is a skill. It involves hard information, experience and intuition. Analysis of the market, the customers, the retailers and the center plays a key role in making successful leasing happen.

Most important, the key to leasing is knowing what can make the deal happen and then knowing how to execute that deal. Creativity and information are the hallmarks of leasing.

The following information will help explain many of the key points about the job of leasing. In so many ways leasing is intuitive, and it is anecdotal. The rules are not always cut and dried, and the keys to success often vary from center to center. But what you—the shopping center professional—will find as you read ahead are many of the concepts and basics that will help you to better understand leasing.

Key words, terms and concepts are clearly defined within the text and also appear in the accompanying glossary.

Acknowledgments

The material in this outline is based in part on a course presented at the International Council of Shopping Centers (ICSC) John T. Riordan School for Professional Development Management Institute.

The International Council of Shopping Centers gratefully acknowledges the individuals mentioned below, who have contributed their expertise to this publication.

Rene F. Daniel, CLS, President, The Daniel Group, LLC
Candace Rice, SCMD, CLS, Group Vice President, Leasing, The Mills Corporation
Richard Wolf, CLS, Senior Vice President, Business Development, DJM Asset Management, LLC

Core Concepts

✓ Income
✓ Center value
✓ Vacancies
✓ Merchandises the center

IMPORTANCE OF LEASING

easing is one of the most important aspects in the overall success of any shopping center. How space is leased, how space for each store is configured, and the deals that are made with each retailer to (1) get them into the center and (2) create a financial arrangement that works for tenant and landlord determine the success or lack of same for the property.

In a general way, the following factors sum up why leasing is so important:

- Without leases a center has no income: If tenants aren't signed up to pay for the space available in the center, there is no cash flow.

- Leases determine the asset value of the center: For example, if you have a one-million-square-foot center with 400,000 square feet of gross leasable area (GLA) and you are able to raise your cash flow by $1 per square foot on each lease, that can mean another $400,000 of income for your center, per year.

- Unleased space means vacancies, and vacancies translate into major management and marketing headaches: Not only is the unleased space unproductive, it takes away from the productivity of all other tenants. Fewer stores mean fewer shoppers, which means fewer sales, which means fewer dollars for everyone.

- Successful leasing works well ahead of the current status of the center: It anticipates market changes, retail evolution and foresees vacancies before they happen. It merchandises the center with the merchandise, food and services your customers want. If you are leasing successfully, you will be predicting many things, including whether:

—Stores need more space
—Stores need less space
—Stores are headed for bankruptcy
—Stores should be let go from the center
—Stores should be brought into the center
—Stores meet the needs of the consumer

Core Concepts

✓ Tenant mix
✓ Center traits and characteristics
✓ Market study
✓ Competition

ORGANIZE FOR EFFECTIVE LEASING

A leasing program requires careful planning and organization. A careful study of all aspects of the center, and the bringing together of all leasing tools, will make the challenge of successful leasing easier to achieve.

Leasing is the process of filling a shopping center with the strongest and best merchants. To accomplish this, there should be an understanding of the center and the tenants who are already there. Before new tenants can be found to fill vacant space, there must be an understanding of the kind of center you have and who its customers are.

Information gained through self-analysis will tell you such things as:

- Where retail gaps exist
- Who is best able to fill any gaps
- What retailers will best complement those already in the center.

Study Your Tenant Mix

Look closely at the tenant mix to see if the center has the right combination of stores.

- Look at the retail categories and the merchandise mix to see if the kind of merchandise carried by those stores is right for the center's market
- Determine if it is high-end, middle of the road, value oriented or something else
- Determine if that mix is working as well as it can.

For example, your center may be too heavy with food vendors and too light in the area of women's ready-to-wear. The merchandise mix may be too rich or not upscale enough for your customer base. It may be aimed at a market that is too old or too young.

Study Your Center's Physical Traits

A shopping center should be understood as a physical plant in order to determine what exactly the center is all about. See how it is configured and which of its spaces are available to be leased. Know all of the physical aspects of the center and how they affect the leasing strategies. For example, you should know about such things as:

- Amount of GLA
- Access to parking
- Number of parking spaces
- Total number of acres on the property site
- Which outparcels are available to lease, and their value
- Zoning problems indigenous to your property
- Restrictions on your property, including sign restrictions
- Location of the center—its county or municipality—and the local officials who may have jurisdiction over the center
- Unusual characteristics about the center that might make leasing more or less difficult
- Layout and specific topographic aspects of the center
- Location of parking levels in relation to the rest of the center and its entrances
- Location of sheer walls (load-bearing walls)
- Age and condition of heating, ventilating and air conditioning (HVAC)
- Heights of the ceilings
- A space's relative proximity to delivery areas
- Location of grease traps for food vendors
- Location of water and sewer lines
- Shapes of vacant spaces
- Availability of a back room that is continuous or contiguous with the space
- Volume of retail shops relative to their size.

Study Your Market

A market study of a center will turn up a wealth of information that can illustrate great changes in the property between the time it was built and the present. These changes can relate to physical aspects of the center's location as well as to demographic differences in the market.

A center's market changes over the years, and these changes must be noted in order for an ongoing leasing program to be successful. For example, a center built 20 years ago may have been surrounded by a development of homes occupied by young couples with children. Over the years, the market may have changed; therefore, the types of stores that should be in the center would have changed. It is important to:

- Be sensitive to market changes.
- Conduct market studies on a regular basis.
- Use the market study to provide insight into the types of retailers the center should be attracting.

The consumer will determine the best retailers to seek out. It is the leasing agent's job to find those retailers. The choice should not depend on the availability of just any retailer who comes along and can pay for an open space. There must be a "fit" that is based on market research and current retail mix in the center.

Study Your Center's Competition

In order to come up with strategies to address the competition head-on, the competition must be thoroughly understood. Know the following facts:

- The closest competition
- The competition's niche in the market
- How what they offer differs from what your center offers
- Market segments where you battle the competition head-on
- Who has joined the competition's roster of tenants.

Keep Detailed Records of Leases

Record keeping is essential to effective leasing activities. These records may include:

- Leasing files: Listings of the tenants' needs and information about how they are performing in the center . . . the history of each tenant's sales.
- Summaries or abstracts on all existing leases: You should know when all leases expire. By combining this information with that of each tenant's business performance, you can plan ahead for the termination or renewal of individual leases. For example, summaries may reveal that a store is too big or too small for the amount of business it is doing or could be doing, provided the space were a correct size.

Prepare for expirations two years in advance to anticipate vacancies.

As you talk to tenants and review their sales, you may be able to tell who is going to go out of business, who needs more or less space and when additional categories should be introduced within the center.

Creativity Assists Leasing

Creative thinking about alternative uses for unusual spaces in the center may help the center make money in spaces where standard tenants will not lease. Uses for these spaces might include:

- Dry cleaners
- Medical/dental clinics
- Schools (for example, beauty or computer)

- Game centers (located, for example, in basements)
- Government offices (located, for example, in poorly exposed spaces)
- Real estate, insurance or tax service offices

These nonretail tenants are more flexible about the spaces they will lease, because they do not depend heavily upon shopper traffic and high visibility to attract business.

Core Concepts

✓ Self-analysis
✓ Prospecting and canvassing
✓ Determining suitability

PROSPECT FOR TENANTS

Tenant prospecting should follow careful self-analysis of your center and its needs.

Managers, leasing agents and marketing directors should keep detailed files on all of their key leasing prospects. These prospects are the potential tenants you define before planning to fill space that comes from vacancies, expirations or the recapturing of space.

Prospecting and canvassing techniques are the homework and legwork you do when looking for appropriate tenants to fill vacancies you have or expect to have in your center.

When canvassing or prospecting for a new tenant to fill a particular retail need, a variety of things can be done. For example, if the center wants a music store tenant, find out:

- What music stores are currently in your market
- Where they are located
- Who the owners are
- If they have any plans for expanding.

The following simple criteria will help build credibility when prospecting:

- Get to know the owners of the stores the center is seeking.
- Develop a list of prospective tenant stores ranging from "best" to "worst."
- Learn as much as possible about each prospect's business.
- Get referrals from merchants about their competitors. When you know the competition, prospects will respect your understanding the full scope of their business.
- Ask questions about the prospects' businesses to build a personal familiarity with what they are facing, what works, what does not work.

Selecting the Best Prospects

When identifying prospective merchants for the center, distinguish the good stores from the bad ones.

To help make a clear and correct identification of who is getting the job done and who is not, observe the following:

- Merchandise setup and general store appearance
- Inventory levels
- Traffic within the store

- Staffing level
- Advertising.

Knowledge of prospects' reputations is essential. Determine the best merchants in each category. Find out what makes them the best. See if they are national, regional or local merchants. Determine which of these classifications fits best in your center to fulfill the center's retail needs.

Shopping centers are a blend of retail offerings. National tenants bring with them a household name and a predictable level of business, but they may lack the exclusivity of quality local merchants.

After determining what a center's retail blend should be, the gaps in the mix can be filled. Tenant prospects should include:

- Enough nationals to give the center the reputation it needs to be successful
- Enough regionals to give it some flavor and strength
- Enough locals to provide some exclusivity.

Core Concepts

✓ Structuring the deal
✓ Rents, CAM and real estate taxes
✓ Percentage and overage rents
✓ T.I. allowances
✓ Gross receipts
✓ Key terminology

THE DEAL

When it comes time to make a deal with a prospective tenant on any retail space, there are two players the leasing person must satisfy—the tenant and the landlord. The tenant is usually willing to pay one price and the landlord may want something else.

The art of making a deal and leasing space is finding the point at which both tenant and landlord are comfortable with what they are giving and getting.

When you enter into negotiations with a prospect, determine a lease structure that will:

- Recognize the potential sales volume of the prospect
- Make co-tenants more profitable

- Provide landlords with greater income
- Stimulate additional leasing activity.

Convince tenants to want the space. Determine the tenant's anticipated sales volume, and then structure the deal around that number to make it work for everyone. The rental should relate to the tenant's level of sales volume.

The Deal Comes Down to Rent

Rent on shopping center retail space can be broken out as:

- Minimum rent: A specific dollar amount paid by the tenant for each square foot of space leased
- Effective rent: The minimum rent and the overage rent (a negotiated percentage of gross sales paid by tenant to landlord after a threshhold of sales known as a breakpoint is exceeded) folded into one
- Additional rent or extras: Additional charges can be a flat charge escalated by consumer price index (CPI) or pro-rata of overall charges. They include common area maintenance (CAM), real estate taxes (RET), insurance, etc. Marketing fund charges are also considered additional rent, thus a part of a retailer's total occupancy charges, but are never billed as a pro-rata portion of landlord's marketing expenses.
- Total rent: The minimum rent, percentage rent and any additional charges, e.g., common area maintenance (CAM), real estate taxes (RET), insurance, marketing fund.

Minimum Rent

Minimum rent can be looked at in a number of ways. In general, there are several varieties of minimum rent:

- Flat rents: A tenant pays a specific monthly charge for a specified number of years. For example, $40 per square foot annually for 10 years.

- Step-up rents: Rents structured so they move up after a specific number of years during the life of the lease. For example, a rent may start at $20 for the first three years, move up to $25 for the next four years and move to $30 for the final three years of the lease.

- Percentage-only rents: These are rents that relate only to a negotiated percentage of a tenant's sales volume. Sometimes these deals are structured so that they convert to a minimum rent at a later date. Percentage-only rents are sometimes referred to as simply "percentage rents" as distinguished from "overage rents," which is the rent the tenant pays in excess of its minimum rent as a percentage of sales that exceeded the breakpoint.

- Free rent: This is a ploy used to attract "hot" tenants to a center and, thereby, attract other tenants to lease the remaining space. For example, tenants will be given a space rent-free for the first year or convert to some form of minimum and/or percentage rent if they sign leases in the center. Free rent is used most often in poorly performing centers.

- Consumer price index increases to minimum rents: Rents that are pegged to rises in the consumer price index and will increase consistent with general cost of living.

Overage Rent/Percentage Rent

Overage rent is paid by tenants in addition to the guaranteed minimum rent they are charged for the square footage leased. Percentage rent represents a percentage of a retailer's total sales for a year, with the percentage negotiated between landlord and tenant. Almost all retail categories have specific and different percentage rental rates. The portion of percentage rent attributed to the additional percentage rent after the breakpoint is reached is known as "overage rent."

EXAMPLE 1

Sales	$220,000
Breakpoint	$200,000
Percentage Rate	5%
Overage Rent	$1,000
*Minimum Rent	$10,000

Formula:

Sales	$220,000
Breakpoint	− $200,000
Overage Sales	$20,000
Percentage Rent	× 5%
Overage Rent	$1,000

*Minimum Rent is stated in the lease. In this case the breakpoint is a "natural breakpoint."

Natural Breakpoint	$200,000
Percentage Rate	× 5%
Minimum Rent	$10,000

The range of percentage rents can vary dramatically, depending on the type of tenant coming into the center. For example, a furniture store with low turnover may pay at the rate of only 2% of sales, while an amusement/game center with higher turnover could pay as much as 15% of gross sales. Apparel typically falls in the 5 to 8% range. The following examples illustrate how sales affect minimum and overage rent using a natural breakpoint.

EXAMPLE 2

ABC Women's Wear Lease
Sales breakpoint: $1,000,000 natural terms square footage 2,000 s.f.
Rent: $60,000 or 6% of sales, whichever is greater
Rent p.s.f.: $30 or 6% of sales, whichever is greater
                (Formula $60,000 ÷ 2,000 s.f. = $30 p.s.f.)
Additional rent: Prorata

EXAMPLE 3

ABC Women's Wear—Current Year

Sales:	$1,200,000	(These are the gross receipts reported by tenant.)
Minimum rent:	$ 60,000	(This amount is fixed, also known as fixed minimum rent (FMR), and may be quoted as $30 per square foot [$60,000 ÷ $2,000 s.f. = $30 p.s.f.])
Percentage rent:	6%	($1,200,000 × 6% = $72,000)
Breakpoint:	$1,000,000	($60,000 fixed minimum rent ÷ 6% percentage rent = $1,000,000 breakpoint.)
Overage sales:	$200,000	($200,000 × 6% = $12,000 overage rent. $1,200,000 sales − $1,000,000 breakpoint = $200,000 overage sales.)
Overage rent:	$12,000	($72,000 total effective rent − $60,000 fixed minimum rent = $12,000 overage rent.)
Effective rent:	$72,000	(When using a natural breakpoint, $1,200,000 total sales × 6% = $72,000 effective rent or $60,000 fixed minimum rent + $12,000 overage rent = $72,000 effective rent.)
Additional rent:	$20,000	($10 × 2,000 s.f. = $20,000)

(CAM $7, RET $2, Mktg. Fund $1 = $10 p.s.f.

Allowances: Construction and Tenant Improvement (T.I.) Allowances

The construction or tenant improvement (T.I.) allowance is something that may be built into a leasing deal to make the deal more attractive. It is something given to the prospective tenant by the landlord, depending upon how much that tenant is wanted for the center. Standard types of construction allowances are:

- Cold dark shell: This is another way of saying the tenant gets a space and nothing else. The *tenant* is responsible for paying all costs of store construction.
- As is: In other words, what you see is what you get. A space exists and it is in a certain state or condition. The landlord may have done some extensive work on the space but will do no more. The space may have been occupied by a previous tenant, and the prospect pays to renovate.
- Negative or reverse allowance (also known as "key money"): Sometimes found in negotiations on food court space. It means the tenant pays a one-time certain amount for the landlord's cost of building the space.
- Turn key: The landlord puts in everything. Tenants generally provide and install their fixtures, show up with their merchandise and are ready for business.
- Vanilla box: A space that is partially completed by the landlord. The work included in a vanilla box depends upon the negotiations between the tenant and the landlord. It typically includes floor, ceiling, lights, walls, HVAC and storefront.
- Fixturing allowance: The landlord gives tenants more money than they need to construct the basic store. This extra money is usually applied to such things as fixtures or merchandise.

- Recapture from overage: Here the landlord allows tenants to recover some or all of their construction costs out of percentage rent paid over a minimum breakpoint. In this case, if the tenant never reaches its breakpoint during the life of the lease, the tenant pays no overage sales and as such is never allowed to recapture its construction allowance. Just how much is allowed and the percentage breaks calculated depend on each negotiation.

EXAMPLE 4

For example:
Tenant is allowed to recover 50% of its $250,000 construction costs during the life of the lease. If in the second year, the tenant pays 6% of rent on its overage sales of $200,000, tenant can recover as follows:

$200,000 × 6% = $ 2,000 overage rent
$250,000 × 50% = $125,000 maximum recapture possible during the life of the lease
$125,000 max. recapture possible − $12,000 recapture from overage rent in year two = $113,000 left to recapture from overage rent during the remaining lease life.

In this example, tenant is allowed to deduct up to 50% of annual real estate taxes from annual overage rent owed, if any:

EXAMPLE 5

	Scenario A	Scenario B	Scenario C
Real Estate Taxes	$2,000	$2,000	$2,000
Overage Rent	0	500	2,000
Deduct up to 50% of Real Estate Taxes as Offset to Overage Rent	0	(500)	(1,000)
Amount Owed	$2,000	$2,000	$3,000

Term of the Lease

The term of the lease is the length of time that a particular lease runs. Length of term depends upon the specific tenant and the negotiations between that tenant and the landlord.

Reduced Rental vs. Vacancy

In some cases, especially when the economy is in poor shape or competition is extremely high, landlords will have to make whatever deals they can, not necessarily those they want to make.

Devices commonly employed by landlords who want to make deals rather than face vacancies include:

- Low rents
- No rents
- Percentage rents only
- Charges only (tenants cover only the common area maintenance (CAM), real estate taxes and insurance charges and utilities they use)
- Conversion of rents (tenants may start at no rent or charges only and then, after a negotiated time or when a level of co-tenancy is reached, e.g., when the center's center section GLA is leased and open by 75% of the space, convert to some rent schedule).

Gross Receipts

In any shopping center lease, when you make a deal with a prospective tenant, there are certain things the tenant may ask for as deductions from percentage rent. These things bring in money and pump up retailers' gross receipts, and thus their percentage rents, but do nothing for the retailers' profitability.

Items which are generally deducted from gross receipts include:

- Returns to shippers: Money coming back to tenant for items returned
- Sale of fixtures and equipment
- Cash or credit refunds
- Exchanges between stores (when they are one for one and do not affect the tenant's true sales)
- Alterations and repairs: Most retailers offer this at little or no profit if it is not their primary business.
- Finance charges
- Employee sales, usually highly discounted
- Bad debts

There are many ways to work around gross receipts to make a deal more attractive to a potential retailer. For example, some jewelry stores, when making credit jewelry sales, also sell insurance policies. This is a service to customers, not always an income producer, and could be knocked out of the retailer's calculation of gross receipts.

By guaranteeing that this would not be calculated, the potential tenant (in this case, a jewelry store) would know that this ancillary aspect of its business would not increase its percentage rent.

Real Estate Taxes

Landlords often treat real estate taxes in much the same way they handle common area maintenance charges. The tenants pay for these taxes through their leases.

The basic ways that landlords charge for real estate taxes follow:

- Pro rata: Tenants pay their pro rata shares of the center's total real estate taxes for its owned parcel, which excludes the parcels that anchors own and pay real estate taxes on. Sometimes tenants will also pay their prorata share of expenses to monitor assessment and contest assessments.
- Increase over a base year: Tenants pay no taxes the first year that establishes their base and will pay increases over that base year.
- Recover from overage: Often used with department stores; tenants recover their tax bills out of what they pay in overage rent. In other words, if their overage rent reaches a certain, negotiated level, they can reduce that overage payment by the amount of their tax bills.
- Stops: Landlords pay taxes up to a certain amount per square foot, and the retailers pay anything over that.

Whether or not these options are used depends upon how much leverage the tenant has with the landlord, how much the landlord wants to make the deal and what it will take to make the deal happen.

Performance Requirements

Landlords write into their leases specific performance requirements that tenants must meet if they are to continue operating in that center. The requirements are negotiated between tenant and landlord and relate directly to the business that the tenant is doing relative to the negotiated expectations.

Performance requirements generally determine one of the following:

- Renewal: If tenants are to be eligible to renew their leases at the date of lease termination, they must achieve a specific volume.
- Canceling after year/performance (also known as "kick out"): Tenants or landlords have the right to cancel leases after specific dates if they do not reach the volume they seek. Sometimes that right to cancel is mutual and can be exercised by either the tenant or the landlord.
- Increasing minimum rent: A landlord may require that base minimum rent be increased if the tenant does not reach a specific volume by a specific date.
- Remodeling requirements: The landlord may state that tenants must remodel their stores after a certain number of years. Definition of what that remodeling is will be spelled out by the landlord.

Common Area Maintenance (CAM)

The landlord will charge the tenants for the cost of maintaining the common area (space that is not leasable but shared by everyone, and helps create an attractive, convenient and comfortable retail environment from which all tenants benefit). Common area may include:

- Walkways (mall area or sidewalks)
- Hallways
- Atriums
- Parking lots
- Rest rooms

Standard ways that landlords charge for CAM include:

- Pro rate: In which tenants pay shares of CAM, based on the size of their retail space plus an administrative fee, typically 15% of CAM

- Flat or fixed rates: All tenants pay a fixed fee regardless of the size of their stores. Certain expenses may be excluded from flat CAM and billed pro-rata, e.g., snow removal

Landlords must keep track of what is included in common area maintenance by paying close attention to all lease clauses. Questions that bear close scrutiny include:

- Does CAM include capital costs of buying machinery used for maintaining the common areas?
- Does CAM include the manager's salary?
- Does CAM include an aministrative fee?
- Are there stores that pay up to a certain amount per square foot in CAM charges and nothing more?
- Can tenants recover any CAM charges from overage?

Use Clauses

The use clause in a shopping center retail lease defines the category of merchandise or items that a retailer is allowed to sell. Use clauses are important factors in any lease negotiation and are invoked for a variety of reasons, among them:

- Importance of control: Use clauses are established in centers to control what tenants sell in their stores and to protect other tenants from having a successful business undermined by another retailer attempting to duplicate that tenant's business.
- Assignment protection: This ensures that retailers who have the right to assign or sell their spaces in the center to other retailers do not deal with tenants whose retail category is deemed inappropriate by the landlord.
- Selected merchandise at lower percentages: Use clauses

may establish that certain types of merchandise be sold at a specific percentage and other types be sold at a different percentage.

Radius Clauses

Radius clauses establish the distance from the center that a retailer can operate another, similar store. Time as well as distance is part of the radius clause. For example, a radius clause may state that a retailer cannot operate another store within three miles of the center for a period of three years.

If such a stipulation is going to hurt a potential deal that the landlord wants, a time element may be added. For example, a retailer may not operate another store within three miles of the center for a negotiated number of years.

In this second example, the radius clause is maintained but softened when a finite amount of time is built into the lease. Therefore, retailers are guaranteed that if all goes well with their businesses, they can open a second one nearby in a certain number of years. The landlord is protected for a given period of time, and the tenant has something to aim for in the future. Penalty for the tenant violating its radius restriction is usually of a monetary nature, e.g., the tenant must report the sales for the additional store along with the sales for the old store and be subject to the original overage sales requirement.

Exclusives

A retailer who enjoys leverage with a specific shopping center may request an exclusive right to sell.

Landlords generally avoid giving exclusives, or mitigate the retailers' requests by showing that the total potential for sales in the retailers' categories well outstrips the rent they are willing to pay—especially if the retailers are paying overage rent.

Co-Tenancy

Tenants may negotiate lease terms that require no minimum rent until a specified percentage of GLA in a center is occupied. Conversely, they may agree to pay full rent until occupancy falls below a certain percentage; if it dips, they may negotiate a lower base rent, may go on a percentage rent basis or be allowed to get out of their lease.

If co-tenancy clauses are written into leases, they may cause a domino effect. For example, a department store leaves or a few retailers go out of business and the center drops below the stated percentage. Then various tenants exercise their rights and leave, and the center suddenly faces a large number of vacancies.

Store Hours

Landlords endeavor to keep store hours throughout their centers consistent and uniform. If some stores close before others and there is no continuity, the lack of regularity could destroy customer loyalty. In general, store hours should not be an area of negotiation in the leasing process.

Exceptions may be made on rare occasions, usually with regard to restaurants or theaters that remain open beyond the regular operating hours of the shopping center.

The Marketing/Promotion Fund vs. Merchants' Association

When looking to establish a mechanism for marketing and promoting a shopping center using funds contributed by the merchants, most centers now utilize a marketing/promotion fund rather than the traditional merchants' association. The marketing fund allows the landlord to determine the distribution of all money pooled for marketing the center.

Merchants' associations are independent bodies made up of merchants' representatives who decide what marketing efforts will be employed by the center. These groups can create situations in which merchants argue about distribution of funds and hold out for their own interests. Marketing funds let the center's marketing staff control the funds and use them for marketing strategies that benefit the entire center.

With a merchants' association, a merchants' committee generally determines how the funds should be spent.

CONCLUSION

Leasing is one of the most important aspects in the overall success of any shopping center. Leases determine income and the productivity of a center. To be effective, a leasing program must be carefully planned and organized. This means studying the tenant mix, the physical plant, the market, the competition, keeping a detailed record of leases and considering creative alternate uses for spaces that are more difficult to lease. When seeking appropriate tenants for vacancies, it's important for the landlord to apply prospecting and canvassing techniques that will result in the best mix for the center. The idea is to negotiate so that the tenant and the landlord are both satisfied with the lease. This can be achieved after considering all sorts of matters—among them rent options, gross receipts, real estate taxes, performance requirements, CAM, co-tenancy—in order to reach the best deal.

Glossary

The glossary that follows is a listing of key definitions compiled from this outline, with several terms not defined in the outline added for your information. The terms are defined within the context of this shopping center management topic.

Asset value   The relative worth of a center based on the net operating income (NOI) that center generates through its leases with tenants and divided by a negotiated capitalization rate. For example:

$$\frac{\$10,000,000 \text{ NOI}}{\div 9 \text{ Cap rate}}$$
$$\$111,111,111 \text{ value}$$

CAM   See Common area maintenance

Cash flow   The amount of spendable income available after all payments have been made for operating expenses and mortgage principal and interest.

Cold Dark Shell   Term for unfinished space leased to a tenant, which the tenant is responsible for paying all costs of construction.

Common area maintenance   The amount of money charged

to tenants for their shares of maintaining a center's common area.

Construction allowance   Money or financial incentives given to tenants for the cost of constructing their store space in a center. Also known as T.I. allowance or tenant improvement allowance.

Co-tenancy   A term that refers to a clause inserted into a tenant's lease stipulating that a reduced rent or no rent be paid until an agreed-upon percentage of the center is occupied. Co-tenancy may also refer to a lease obligation that depends on another store being open for business, such as a department store.

CPI rents   Rents that are pegged to rises in the consumer price index.

Demographics   The statistical characteristics of population groups, sorted out by such things as age and income, used to identify markets.

Effective rent   A combination of the minimum and percentage (overage) rent paid by a tenant.

Exclusives   A term referring to a store's being given the exclusive right to sell a particular category of merchandise within a shopping center.

Flat rents   A specific rent on square footage paid by a tenant for a specified period of time.

Gross leasable area (GLA)   The square footage of a shopping center that can generate income by being leased to tenants. These can include anchor space if the anchor leases from the landlord.

High end   Refers to tenants offering better quality and/or exclusive merchandise at higher prices.

HVAC   An acronym that stands for heating, ventilating and air-conditioning. Used in reference to the groupings of these systems in any shopping center.

Key money   Money from the tenant to the landlord for the right to operate a business in the center.

Local tenant   A retail tenant who operates one or more stores exclusively in a local market, but is not regional or national in scope. For example, a tenant that operates four stores only in the Miami/Ft. Lauderdale MSA is a local tenant, whereas a tenant that operates four stores in that market plus one store in Tampa and one in Orlando is a regional tenant.

Marketing/promotion fund   The pooling and distribution of money paid by tenants for the overall marketing of the shopping center. The marketing/promotion fund is overseen by the center's marketing director and staff and is used for advertising and promotion activities.

Market study   A comprehensive analysis of a center's consumer market. The customers, the demographics and the competition are all components of a market study.

Merchandise mix   The variety and categories of merchandise offered by the retail tenants assembled in a particular shopping center.

Minimum rent   The specific fixed minimum rent dollar amount paid by a tenant for the amount of square footage leased, notwithstanding an obligation to pay overage rent if sales exceed a breakpoint.

Mom-and-pop store   A store whose owners own only that single store.

National tenant   A retailer who operates a chain of stores on a nationwide basis, not necessarily in all states but substantially from coast to coast.

Nonretail tenants   Shopping center tenants, primarily service-oriented tenants, who do not fit into the traditional category of retailers; a tenant selling services, not goods.

Outparcels   Unused portions of a shopping center's site that constitute the perimeter areas, not including the center facility or parking lot, that may be used or developed for similar or nonsimilar purposes.

Regional tenant   A retailer who operates stores in a particular region of the country. This can be within one state or province or within several states or provinces.

Radius clause   A clause inserted into a shopping center retail lease establishing the distance from the center that the retailer may operate another, similar store.

Reverse allowance   The tenant pays a one time specific amount of money over any minimum and percentage rents for the landlord's cost of building the space. Also known as key money.

Step rents Rents that are structured so they increase at specific times during the life of a lease.

Total rent The minimum and percentage rent paid by a tenant, coupled with any extra charges that the tenant must pay. Also known as total occupancy cost and may be expressed as a percentage of sales, e.g., XYZ Women's Wear pays 10% in total occupancy costs in line with other women's apparel stores.

Traffic The number or volume of shoppers who visit a shopping center during a specified period of time.

Turn key Landlord builds and finishes out a retail space; tenant shows up with fixtures and merchandise and is ready for business.

Use clause A clause inserted into a shopping center retail lease that defines the category of merchandise or items that a retailer is allowed to sell.

Vanilla box A space partially completed by the landlord based on negotiations between tenant and landlord. Although every landlord's definition is different, a vanilla box normally includes HVAC, walls, floors, stockroom wall, basic electrical work, basic plumbing work, rear door and storefront.